BEST BIBLE STORIES

The Baby in the Basket

THE BABY IN THE BASKET

Jennifer Rees Larcombe

Illustrated by Steve Björkman

CROSSWAY BOOKS • WHEATON, ILLINOIS
A DIVISION OF GOOD NEWS PUBLISHERS

The Baby in the Basket
Text copyright © 1992, 1997 by Jennifer Rees Larcombe
Illustrations copyright © 1997 by Steve Björkman
U. S. edition published 1999 by Crossway Books
a division of Good News Publishers
1300 Crescent Street
Wheaton, Illinois 60187
First British edition published 1992
by Marshall Pickering as part of *Children's Bible Story Book.*
This book published as a separate edition in 1997
by Marshall Pickering, an Imprint of HarperCollins Religious,
part of HarperCollins Publishers,
77-85 Fulham Palace Road, London W6 8JB.
Cover design: Cindy Kiple
First U. S. printing 1999
Printed in Hong Kong
ISBN 1-58134-055-9

THE BABY IN THE BASKET

Exodus 1; 2:2–10

"Who **are** all those people?" stormed Pharaoh the King of Egypt as his boat floated down the Nile River. "They're not Egyptians!"

"No, your Majesty," replied his butler,

"they are Jews." The Jews were God's very

own people, and they had been living in Egypt for
hundreds of years.

"I don't like them!" said Pharaoh angrily.

"There are far too many of them, and they're living on the best land in my kingdom. Just look at all their fat sheep eating my grass!

I'll have to get rid of them. They might fight against us Egyptians one day, and anyway I want to build on their land."

"You shall be our

slaves!"

he shouted angrily
across the water.
"You'll work so hard
you'll

soon die."

Day after day, in the blistering sun, the poor Jews were bullied by Egyptians with great whips. They hardly had any food as they were forced to build cities, palaces and pyramids.

"There are **still** too many of them," muttered Pharaoh. **"Soldiers,"** he ordered, "every time a Jewish baby boy is born, throw it into the river!"

"Oh God, help us!" cried the poor Jews, and

God heard them.

One day in a little slave hut, a very special baby was born.

"We **can't** let him be drowned," sobbed his mother, "but if we keep him here the soldiers are bound to hear him cry."

So they made a floating cradle for Moses, out of a waterproof basket. In the morning, long before anyone was awake, they crept down to the river and hid the basket in the reeds. Miriam, the baby's big sister, was left to guard him.

The gentle lapping of the water soon rocked Moses to sleep, and Miriam began to weave a mat of reeds.

Then, suddenly, she was **stiff with fear.**

Someone was coming.

Down the path from the palace came the Princess, Pharaoh's own daughter. Poor Miriam was shaking with fright as she watched the Princess slide into the water for a swim.

"Wade over and get me that funny little basket," said the Princess to one of her maids, and Miriam closed her eyes in horror.

"Oh look!" exclaimed the Princess. "It's a darling little Jewish baby. I won't let Father drown him; he shall be mine for always."

Just at that moment Moses began to cry loudly.
"Oh dear!" said the Princess
doubtfully. "He's probably hungry."

Quickly Miriam slipped out of her hiding place and said, "Would you like me to find someone to look after your baby for you?"

"Thank you," said the Princess. She was pleased to find someone to feed the baby.

Of course Miriam ran straight to fetch her mother, who looked after Moses as he grew up in the royal palace.

She told him the secret about the beautiful land God had promised to give his people one day.

"You must grow up to be a Prince that follows God, my son," she would whisper.

"Perhaps He will use you to save your people from being slaves and take them back to their own land."

Let's talk about the story

1. Why did Pharaoh want to get rid of the Jews?

2. What happened when the Jews prayed?

3. How did Moses' parents keep him alive?

4. Why was Moses a very special baby?

5. God gives each one of us gifts and talents to use for Him. Name some of the talents He gave you.

6. God has a special plan for everyone, no matter how young or old. What special plans might He have for you right now?